27 MILLION ADULTS
IN THE UK PRAY.
10 MILLION PRAY REGULARLY.
HALF OF THOSE WHO
PRAY BELIEVE GOD HEARS
THEIR PRAYERS.
OF PEOPLE WHO SAY
THEY ARE NOT RELIGIOUS
1 IN 5 PRAY.[1]

Need help?

People have health scares and worry about relationships and the future. People stress about money and suffer from depression.

You could find the help you have been missing.

Missing something?

Even with a full life we can feel empty and wonder if there is more to life than this.

You could begin the adventure of a lifetime.

Curious?

You don't have to have a problem to pray. Many people simply want to know if there is something that can make sense of life.

You could discover new possibilities.

THE MORNING OF A JOB INTERVIEW. THE NIGHT WHEN A FAMILY MEMBER IS SICK. THE FIVE MINUTES BEFORE AN EXAM. MOST PEOPLE HAVE PRAYED IN MOMENTS OF DESPERATION. WAS SOMEONE LISTENING? WAS THE PRAYER ANSWERED? PEOPLE FIND PRAYING HELPS AND HAVE HAD ANSWERS.

YOU CAN FIND OUT IF SOMEONE DOES LISTEN AND CARE.

BIG ISSUE?

Do you have a 'big issue?'
This is something that you really
want God to do something about.

Pray about this each day and see
what happens. Is there someone
you're concerned about?

Why not pray for them –
or with them – during this week?

PRAYER IS A CONVERSATION WITH GOD. YOU DON'T NEED TO USE SPECIAL WORDS OR A SPECIAL VOICE. YOU CAN PRAY OUT LOUD OR SILENTLY. GOD KNOWS WHAT YOU THINK AND IS AWARE OF ALL YOU DO. YOU CAN TALK TO HIM ABOUT ANYTHING.

TRY PRAYING FOR 7 DAYS

What to do

Find a time and a place that will suit you. Read this booklet one day at a time. Try to keep going for a week, but don't feel guilty if you miss a day. You might like to tell a friend you are doing this and talk about how it is going.

'GOD, IF YOU ARE THERE –
AND I AM NOT SURE YOU
ARE – BUT IF YOU ARE,
I WANT TO KNOW YOU.
I DON'T WANT TO FOOL
MYSELF; I REALLY WANT TO
KNOW YOU. SO AS I PRAY,
PLEASE MAKE YOURSELF
KNOWN TO ME.'

WISE WORDS

Here's a piece of a conversation between Jesus and a man who wanted his son to be healed – encouragement from Jesus and honesty from the father. Jesus said,

'EVERYTHING IS POSSIBLE FOR ONE WHO BELIEVES.' IMMEDIATELY THE BOY'S FATHER EXCLAIMED, 'I DO BELIEVE; HELP ME OVERCOME MY UNBELIEF.'[2]

Impossible

Anyone there?

Maybe God is closer than you think. Imagine a conversation between twins in the womb. Stupid idea, because they can't talk. But go with it for a minute:

One says, 'We've got a mother who has made us and is all around us. One day we will meet her.'

The other says, 'I'm not so sure about this idea of a mother. I don't think there is anything outside this life. We've got all we need and we've got each other. There is nothing more than we can see and feel here. I find the idea of having 'a mother' rather unscientific, amusing in fact.'

Whether they believe in a mother or not their world will soon be shaken by enormous contractions.

Ok, illustrations are limited, but the point is someone is closer than you think. There's an old saying that 'In him (God) we live and move and have our being.'

People often struggle to find God in their lives, but the truth is he's all around us. We can reach out for him and find him because, in fact, he is not far from anyone.

God is interested in us and we are in some way made like him – in his image. It makes knowing him a genuine option.

TRY PRAYING

God, it feels a little strange talking to you, but I'm giving it a go. Perhaps you are closer than I think. If that's true then I'm not going to ask for a sign, but I am going to ask that you will remove anything that stops me from seeing you.

TRY THIS

Something you can do today...

Phone

Every time you pick up your phone, pray:
'God, I need communication with you.'

Your big issue

If you have an issue in your life in which
you need God to make a difference, pray about
it. Ask him about it right now. Be encouraged –
all things are possible with God.

Have you a friend or family member who needs
help? Why not pray for them each day this week
as well?

Something happened

David Hill, entrepreneur

I was a student, studying Maths at university. I considered myself an agnostic, but I was provoked by the confidence of some Christians I met. I argued with them for many months. I became persuaded there was more evidence about Jesus than I had thought.

I was not being asked to trust something flaky but to trust something that was convincing. As yet, I was not quite sure, but maybe Jesus had lived. Maybe Jesus had risen from the dead. Months passed but eventually I got to the point of giving it a go. With Maths books in front of me in the university library, I prayed, asking Jesus to make himself real to me. It was an important decision and I expected something to happen. But nothing did.

Two weeks later I prayed again – I made the decision to believe in God. I suppose that was when I trusted him with my life. The next day something unusual happened. Alone in my room I experienced a quiet and undeniable assurance that Jesus was alive and that his Spirit was in my life. The experience became overwhelming, lasting several hours. I hadn't known feelings like it. It was from then on that life began to change. God had begun to answer my prayer.

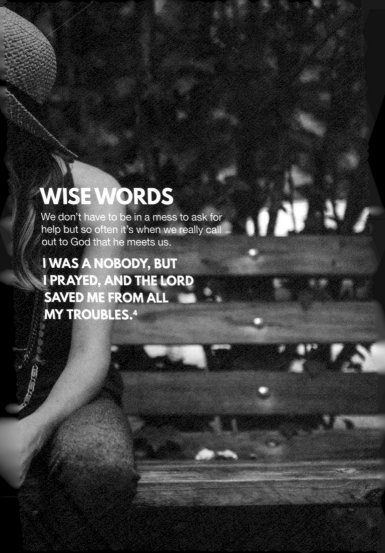

WISE WORDS

We don't have to be in a mess to ask for help but so often it's when we really call out to God that he meets us.

I WAS A NOBODY, BUT I PRAYED, AND THE LORD SAVED ME FROM ALL MY TROUBLES.[4]

Nerve

Imagine what would happen if you went to a friend in the middle of the night and said, 'Can you lend me some bread? Someone has just turned up and I don't have anything to give him.' But your friend answers, 'Don't bother me; we're all in bed. The door is locked, the children are asleep; I can't get up and give you anything.'

But if you show some nerve and keep knocking, risking waking the neighbours, even if he won't get up because he is your friend, he'll finally get up and give you whatever you need because of your persistence.

This scene was described by Jesus centuries ago. He was really talking about prayer: 'Here's what I am saying: Ask and it will be given to you; seek and you will find; knock and the door will be opened to you.

'For everyone who asks receives; the one who seeks finds; and to the one who knocks, the door will be opened.'

Jesus then went on to say this: 'Which of you fathers, if your son asks for a fish, will give him a snake instead? Or if he asks for an egg, will give him a scorpion? If you then, though you are evil, know how to give good gifts to your children, how much more will your father in heaven give the Holy Spirit to those who ask him!'[3]

When we find ourselves in a tight spot we should keep on praying believing God gives good things. So ask!

TRY PRAYING

God I want to understand this idea of persistence. I need you to do something in a number of areas of my life. So I'm asking you to give answers. And I'm choosing to believe you are good and you only give good things.

TRY THIS

Something you can do today...

Stone

Carry a stone with you and every time you put your hand on it pray, 'God, I want you to be the solid thing in my life.'

Keep praying for

Your big issue – the area in your life where you most want God to work.

Others – your friend or family member who needs help – perhaps especially with the idea of finding meaning to life.

How do we pray?
See page 38–39

Something happened

Julia Clapp, youth worker

On a trip to Ibiza I fell into conversation with a holiday maker who was limping. He happened to be a doctor. As we talked he said he wasn't sure whether or not he believed in God; more particularly he didn't think God was concerned about him. But he told me he had really hurt his foot that day and was finding it difficult to walk. He thought he had broken his toes and as he was a doctor he probably had quite a good idea.

I summoned my courage and asked him if I could pray with him for God to heal his foot. He kept saying he was unsure about that because God had bigger things to deal with. Nevertheless I told him that I thought God would love to heal him and that I would pray for him later, which I did shortly afterwards.

About an hour later that same night I saw him again. He made a point of coming over to talk.

He told me something had happened. Quite incredibly, his foot had got much better which he demonstrated by standing on tip toe – quite a difference from earlier! He was astounded and even went as far as to say it was miracle. He said he would have to 'look into God' when he got home.

I learned a lot from this. I've gone from thinking God might heal to knowing he can.

WISE WORDS

This is what Jesus said he came to do.
It's his manifesto:

THE SPIRIT OF THE LORD IS ON ME, BECAUSE HE HAS ANOINTED ME TO PREACH GOOD NEWS TO THE POOR. HE HAS SENT ME TO PROCLAIM FREEDOM FOR THE PRISONERS AND RECOVERY OF SIGHT FOR THE BLIND, TO RELEASE THE OPPRESSED, TO PROCLAIM THE YEAR OF GOD'S FAVOUR.[5]

Quality

There's got to be something better

We live in a rich country but we're not happy. We've accumulated huge levels of debt. Sexual freedom has brought about the disintegration of family life. We're eating and drinking ourselves to death. Mental health problems are rife.

Are we missing something? Is there another way of living life?

20 centuries ago Jesus' first words were an invitation to live life differently. He invited people to change their thinking because there was a new world order about to break in. He said that heaven was coming to earth – in fact had already come. It was beginning through him and would roll down the centuries through the lives of people who followed him.

It is estimated that there are 2.3 billion people who have some loyalty towards Christ today – more than any other world religion and still increasing. But becoming religious is not the point. What matters is that we become part of this movement for change.

Jesus had a manifesto (see opposite). It was what he wanted to do for people. Heaven was poised to affect human lives – positively. Jesus' invitation to 'change our lives because God's kingdom is here' remains as contemporary and relevant as ever.

Heaven is knocking at your door, not to condemn you, but to give you a new quality of life!

TRY PRAYING

God, I recognise that the world has gone wrong in many ways and I want to be part of something better. I'm sorry for my own part in making things go wrong. Make me someone who is connected with heaven.

TRY THIS

Something you can do today...

Key

Every time you use a key today, pray,
'God, unlock my life to your influence.'

Keep praying for

Your big issue – the area in your life where you most
want God to work.

Others – your friend or family member who
needs help.

Something happened

East Germany

1989 was the year that the Berlin wall came down and 10 East European nations were released from communist rule. Historians will cite many reasons for this change. However one factor is overlooked: a prayer meeting in Leipzig.

For 40 years people in East Germany had been longing for better things. In 1982 Pastor Christian Fuehrer started praying with a few people in his Leipzig church. Seven years later four churches were holding weekly prayer meetings, and the numbers began to grow, attracting ordinary citizens. After the meetings, candlelit peace marches through the city took place.

The communist authorities debated how they could stamp it out. The secret police issued death threats and roughed up some of the marchers. But the crowds kept coming. Eventually as many as 50,000 came.

On 9th October 1989, police and army units moved into Leipzig. People feared a massacre and hospital emergency rooms were cleared. Honecker, the East German leader, gave permission to use force, but the prayer meeting and the march went ahead. 70,000 people marched; the following Monday 120,000, and a week later 500,000.

People marched in other cities, including 1 million in East Berlin. Then something amazing happened. Following a Government announcement, crowds flocked to the border. People started crossing to West Berlin without a shot being fired. The Berlin wall and all it symbolised had just crumbled.

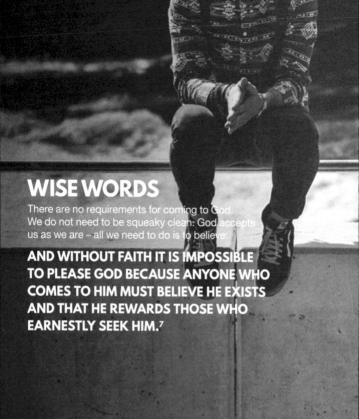

WISE WORDS

There are no requirements for coming to God.
We do not need to be squeaky clean: God accepts
us as we are – all we need to do is to believe:

**AND WITHOUT FAITH IT IS IMPOSSIBLE
TO PLEASE GOD BECAUSE ANYONE WHO
COMES TO HIM MUST BELIEVE HE EXISTS
AND THAT HE REWARDS THOSE WHO
EARNESTLY SEEK HIM.**[7]

Faith

There was a woman who had been ill for ages. She had tried all the help the doctors could offer and spent all her money in the process. But this particular gynaecological problem was not going away. She had one last hope. Jesus had been healing all sorts of people from all sorts of problems. Perhaps, she thought, he could sort her condition.

So she mingled with the crowds around Jesus as he was going to see someone. There were many people and she didn't want to draw attention to herself, but she pushed through the crowds, reached out and caught Jesus' cloak. Suddenly she knew she wasn't ill any more.

Jesus said it was her faith that healed her.

She believed he could make the difference in her life. But she had to do something. She showed her faith by going to him and touching him. That was when power came out of him to heal her.[6]

Faith is what makes the difference between the many that just hang around and the one who really connects.

TRY PRAYING

Jesus, there is something about you that challenges me. I'm being encouraged to put my faith in you but I don't find that easy. I'm on the fence and I want to get off on the right side. I like what I know of you, so I am choosing to trust you now.

TRY THIS

Something you can do today...

Walk

As soon as you start walking from your home pray, 'God, please walk through the day with me.'

Keep praying for

Your big issue – the area in your life where you most want God to work.

Others – your friend or family member who needs help.

What about unanswered prayer?
See page 42–43

Something happened

Nyree, young mum

When my youngest child Jonah was only a few months old I developed an infection related to breast-feeding. The infection ran the whole way through my body.

There were so many things I couldn't do. The kids couldn't hug me any more. I couldn't lift the buggy. On top of all that, I'd pulled muscles in my chest wall.

I went to hospital, but they told me there was nothing they could do – I just had to go home and take complete bed rest. They said the illness would heal up within six months.

So life was pretty tough, and I knew that I needed God to heal me. A couple from the church came round to pray and as they prayed with me, light just flooded through my body.

All I could see was bright light. From that day on, the infection was gone and didn't return.

But I still had terrible pain so the couple from church came again. The second time they prayed with me, it was like this light went right through my body. The pain left and it didn't come back. I was able to carry on feeding the baby and look after the kids as normal. It was amazing. I thank God that he did this for me.

WISE WORDS

From an ancient prayer here's a rich statement of what God is like:

BUT YOU, O LORD, ARE A COMPASSIONATE AND GRACIOUS GOD, SLOW TO ANGER, ABOUNDING IN LOVE AND FAITHFULNESS. TURN TO ME...[8]

And here is what Jesus taught us to pray:

FORGIVE US OUR SINS, AS WE ALSO FORGIVE EVERYONE WHO SINS AGAINST US.[9]

Credit

People make a lot of Jesus dying on the cross. So a good man dies a horrible death. That's happened to many others. What's so special about him?

The reason it was special is because Jesus died for a purpose. Most people know they'll die, but not many say they'll die for the sake of others. Yet Jesus said this many times. He would give up his life because of his love for people. In an unusual way his death was like paying a ransom to get people out of a fix. The 'fix' is serious. People are loved by God but are not living the way he intended. As a result we've run out of credit and are in significant moral debt – with eternal consequences.

Jesus' death was a way of writing off our debt. God himself – in the person of Jesus – paid the ultimate price to set people free.

How does it work? It is something of a mystery. But as Jesus was a perfect human – the God/man – he entered death on behalf of the human race and emerged from it alive again. Like a football team representing a nation, Jesus represented the human race. He endured and defeated the worst thing imaginable, the judgement hanging over us, so we can be free.

It was so impressive that those who witnessed him dying said this man really was the Son of God. A writer at the time explained it saying 'God proves his love for us in that while we were still sinners Christ died for us.'

The result is astounding. Instead of being in debt we are freed, forgiven and in credit. People have been in awe of this demonstration of God's love ever since.

TRY PRAYING

God, if you really did die for me then the least I can say is thank you. I'm sorry for my failure to do what's right. Thank you for your love for me and for forgiving me.

TRY THIS

Something you can do today...

Draw

Take a piece of paper and write on it anything you
feel ashamed about. Then draw a cross over all you
have written and thank Jesus for paying your debt.
(When you have finished shred the paper!).

Keep praying for

Your big issue – the area in your life where you
most want God to work.

Others – your friend or family member who
needs help.

Why is there so much suffering?
See page 40–41

Something happened

Bonny, social worker

As a child I suffered years of abuse. Even into my thirties I had flashbacks of the terrible things I suffered. Years of hating people who had hurt me left me with a very bitter heart. I was often ill with physical and mental pain. I was in complete distress.

Having become a Christian at the age of 31 the issue of forgiving those who hurt me reared its head. I did not want to do this. I recall banging my fists on the floor and telling God in no uncertain terms that I would not and could not forgive.

But as time went on I began to realise forgiveness was not about those who had hurt me. It was about the damage that not forgiving was doing to me. I learned that forgiving is a decision I could make, not a feeling I should feel.

So I said these words, 'God I do not feel like forgiving but as an act of my will I choose to forgive. I ask that you forgive the people who hurt me and forgive me for all the wrong things I have done.'

An amazing thing then happened. As I forgave, God took away the dreadful flashbacks and pain I had felt all those years. The flashbacks began to get less and less and the physical pain in my body began to heal.

I now know that God can rewrite a life no matter how sad or painful it has been.

WISE WORDS

These words have been the invitation to which millions have responded through the centuries. They come directly from Jesus and are an astonishing offer to get to know him:

HERE I AM! I STAND AT THE DOOR AND KNOCK. IF ANYONE HEARS MY VOICE AND OPENS THE DOOR, I WILL COME IN AND EAT WITH THEM AND THEY WITH ME.[10]

Spark

The ignition spark on the oven just wasn't doing anything. It was supposed to deliver the spark to the gas and then we could get cooking. But nothing. All the hardware was there. The oven, the gas rings, the gas connected. But no spark. It had become clogged with years of dirt and grease. It needed a clean.

Life. It's all there, but the spark is missing. As far as human beings are concerned we are not fully alive until we have the 'spark' of God's Holy Spirit in our lives. We were never meant to live life without him. It's as senseless as trying to cook without power. How do we get the spark?

Become religious? No. Pray hard? No. Go to church? No. None of these deal with the issue. We need to get rid of the dirt and press the 'ignition' button.

How? Don't cover up the dirt, but get rid of it. There's stuff that has spoiled your life – the grime and dirt has built up.

You can be clean by asking God to forgive you for the wrong you have done. Admit it and say sorry.

Then ask for God's Spirit to come to your life to make you what you were meant to be. He comes to live in us, empowering us to be what we should be. He makes us truly alive.

TRY PRAYING

God, I'm sorry for things that have spoiled my life. I must have offended you in it all as well. Please forgive me and help me to forgive myself. I ask that you would come into my life right now through your Spirit and make me the kind of person you want me to be.

TRY THIS

Something you can do today...

Door

Go to your front door and say to Jesus,
'Please enter my life today. You are welcome.'

Keep praying for

Your big issue – the area in your life where
you most want God to work.

Others – your friend or family member
who needs help.

So what about the Holy Spirit?
See page 37

Something happened

Wilson, quality inspector

I suppose I had little or no interest in religion. I was happily married. I was not averse to a few drinks and had gradually become a heavy drinker.

One day my wife Lesley said she had something to tell me. She said she'd become a Christian. "Wow," I thought, "where'd that come from?" I started to notice small changes in her. It got me curious.

I was still sceptical but was wondering if God was really there. A year later I was given a copy of the trypraying booklet. I read it from cover to cover in one go. When I finished reading I put the booklet down and did something I will never regret, I simply looked up and said to God: 'Hello?'

Looking back, that first prayer started me on a journey that has brought a lot of change. The journey involved going to a meeting to find out more, attending an Alpha course and responding to an invitation to come closer to Jesus. I opened my life to him.

On one occasion I had an amazing experience of God's Spirit where wave after wave of all I can describe as pure love, began to wash over me, again and again.

I said to Lesley, "It's all true. He's real," to which she replied; "I told you he was".

I'm no longer a heavy drinker.

WISE WORDS

This life is not all there is and a bright future awaits those who believe. These words give us a glimpse of things to come:

NO EYE HAS SEEN, NO EAR HAS HEARD, NO MIND HAS CONCEIVED WHAT GOD HAS PREPARED FOR THOSE WHO LOVE HIM.[14]

Awe

When God breaks through, people are awestruck. Life is never the same again. They see something that was always there, but they had never noticed. A process of change begins which affects how they think and what they do.

The Bible is full of stories of people who had experiences of God. One man describes what he saw and heard. It was so profound and real that the doorposts of the building shook and the place was filled with smoke. He writes, 'I saw God, seated on a throne – high, exalted.' He saw other beings and heard words being called out, 'Holy, holy, holy, is God almighty, the whole earth is full of his glory.' He realised that God was holy and that, in stark contrast, he and his society were foul mouthed and sinful.[11]

Another man describes a common experience: being overwhelmed by love.

He writes, 'Hope does not disappoint us, because God has poured out his love into our hearts by the Holy Spirit, whom he has given us.'[12]

Many people think that the consequence of following Jesus is a life that is boring and dull. So they are stunned by his words when he said he had come to give life and life to the full.[13]

We may not have a dramatic experience of God. We certainly cannot demand it. But knowing that he loves us, and that he is holy, has a profound effect on us. They are the foundation of a relationship with him that changes our whole life now.

TRY PRAYING

God I would like to have an experience of your love. I want to live my life with you, trusting your love and knowing that you are holy.

TRY THIS

Something you can do today...

Look

Go to a place where you can see a view and pray, 'God you are bigger than this world and bigger than my biggest thought of you. So I want you to be the biggest thing in my life.'

Keep praying for

Your big issue – the area in your life where you most want God to work.

Others – your friend or family member who needs help.

Something happened

Overflowing

During the Welsh Revival in 1904, a man called Joseph Kemp from Edinburgh went to Wales, where he spent a couple of weeks observing and experiencing the work and power of the Holy Spirit there.

On his return he attended a large meeting in an Edinburgh church. As he recounted his experiences, there was an eager response to his story. A man asked for prayer and was the first of hundreds who became Christians during the subsequent revival. For a whole year, prayer meetings were held, increasing in number and intensity, and characterised by passionate praying.

An account of one meeting reports that the fire of God fell. A sudden overwhelming sense of his reality, his all-powerful presence and of eternal things was experienced.

'Prayer and weeping began, and gained in intensity every moment. Friends who were gathered sang on their knees. Each seemed to sing, and each seemed to pray, oblivious of one another…

'Then the prayer broke out again, waves and waves of prayer, and the midnight hour was reached. The hours had passed like minutes. It is useless being a spectator looking on, or praying for it in order to catch its spirit and breath. It is necessary to be in it, praying in it, part of it, caught by the same power, swept by the same wind.'

One who was present says: 'I cannot tell you what Christ was to me last night. My heart was full to overflowing. If ever my God was near to me, it was last night.'

Next

If you have discovered something during this week then keep going! You've just started and it gets better. The main thing is to get to know more and more of God. You might like to:

- Tell a friend about your experiences. If they are not interested find a friend that is!

- Get more of the story. Read the Bible. It's full of wisdom for living and hope for the next life. Begin with the accounts of the life of Jesus. You'll be impressed.

- Keep praying with a 40 day prayer guide – 'Catching the Wave'. Visit 40-days.com to find out more.

- Check out some good web sites. Several are listed on www.trypraying.co.uk which also gives access to the trypraying app.

- Go on a course. There are many good introductory courses like Alpha, Christianity Explored, etc. See what is on offer locally.

- Check out a good church. You may need to try a few before you find one that's right for you. Find one that helps you connect with Jesus.

Holy Spirit?

Listen to the things people talk about today and it is often full of spiritual stuff, whether getting in touch with your inner self, spirit guides or mysterious experiences. Dive into almost any civilisation and people are aware of the spiritual, even in our secular materialistic world.

However the Holy Spirit is something else. Clear teaching from Jesus shows us that the Spirit is not an 'it' but a person. In fact Jesus told his followers that the Spirit would come and be his presence with them. After he rose from the dead he told them to wait until he – the Holy Spirit – had come. They would be given power and led into truth through the Holy Spirit.

Today when someone trusts Christ with their life, the Spirit comes to them as a sort of deposit on all the good things that are still to come.

He is the essence of God dwelling in us. The effect of this is that he makes us aware when we have done wrong and in a special way he lets us know, on the inside, that we are loved and belong to God as his children.

Ask for God's Spirit to work in you.

How to pray?

Praying isn't just for the religious. Most people admit to praying at some time in their life even if they have given up on it later.

Jesus prayed. He seemed to have access to God like no one else. He was always doing miracles and teaching about life. But he also spent much time in prayer and taught about it. What did he say?

He said that faith was a crucial ingredient. He always responded to faith. On one occasion he said, 'Therefore I tell you, whatever you ask for in prayer, believe that you have received it and it will be yours.'[15] Prayer is not simply about the words we say, it's about what we are thinking on the inside.

Jesus also said that forgiveness was important. 'And whenever you stand praying, if you hold anything against anyone, forgive them so that your Father in heaven may forgive you'[16]. Forgiveness is a kind of currency. If we use it in our relationship with others then we will have it in our relationship with God.

Another ingredient is to keep going. He gave many illustrations about this: a woman keeping on at a magistrate until he granted her request[17]; a friend banging on the door at midnight until he got what he needed.[18] It seems that praying for something until we get it is what God invites us to do. Giving up at the first set back is not an option.

We have to be willing to accept God's answers when they come which of course can be 'yes', 'no' or 'wait'. Submitting our lives to his will is really the best thing for us. Praying with others and in agreement with them are other principles.

Perhaps we should check that there is nothing in our lives which offends God. If we cling to wrongdoing in an area of our life then he will not hear our prayer.[19] We can't claim to know God and live a life which is at odds with that relationship.

But the foundation for all prayer is knowing God in a personal way. That is what Jesus has made possible.

Ask and it will be given to you.

Suffering?

**War. Oppression.
Earthquakes. Viruses.
Cancer. Poverty Death.
Where is the good news
in the midst of all
this suffering?**

There is a prayer which has
come to us from the first
century. It was taught by
Jesus to his followers and
became known as the Lord's
Prayer (printed opposite). A
phrase in it is, 'Your kingdom
come, your will be done on
earth as it is in heaven.'

It's a powerful request which
Jesus included so that we ask
for something better on earth.

It's fascinating because it
completely turns on its head
a common misunderstanding:
when things go wrong,
people blame God. When
suffering occurs people
often think it is God's will.

But what Jesus said kicks
that into touch. He says
God's will is often NOT
being done! It's a mess and
God is not happy with it.

This kind of language confirms
that things are not right. We
live on a beautiful planet, but
bad stuff happens – really bad
stuff. We are a flawed human
race. At times we do appalling
things that bring suffering to
others. These things definitely
aren't in line with God's will.

In addition, Jesus mentions
circumstances and influences
that test us and he says
there is an 'evil one'.

So instead of laying the
blame for bad stuff at God's
door we should put blame
where it really belongs.

'Your kingdom come!'

We are invited to pray for
God's kingdom to come;
something which will make
life on earth better.

We can ask that things here would change and for God's will to be done instead.

God's ultimate purposes will be fulfilled and he will right all wrongs. Not only that, but he is not uncaring as we face suffering but he is compassionate. He understands our suffering and will come alongside us, to comfort.

The Lord's Prayer

This, then, is how you should pray:

'OUR FATHER IN HEAVEN, HALLOWED BE YOUR NAME, YOUR KINGDOM COME, YOUR WILL BE DONE ON EARTH AS IT IS IN HEAVEN. GIVE US TODAY OUR DAILY BREAD. FORGIVE US OUR DEBTS, AS WE ALSO HAVE FORGIVEN OUR DEBTORS. AND LEAD US NOT INTO TEMPTATION, BUT DELIVER US FROM THE EVIL ONE.'

Unanswered Prayer?

A man prayed for his son's epilepsy to stop. It didn't. Years of uncontrollable seizures robbed his son of language and ability. In another family, prayer for a deaf boy left him unchanged. Elsewhere, a good relationship spiralled into an abusive one and, in spite of prayer, separation was the outcome.

Where is God when he doesn't answer?

Prayer is a conversation between friends. It's not like sending an email off into cyberspace wondering if it will ever be read by someone. If we are in a friendship with Jesus Christ we can be sure our prayers are heard. Fundamentally it is less about 'getting something' and more about 'knowing someone'. Our needs often propel us deeper into a relationship with God.

There are times when we just need to keep going, knowing that it is not yet the end of the story. There's an old African proverb that says, 'No situation stays forever'. Often perplexing situations of unanswered prayer will gradually change as we persist.

Some things don't work out the way we wanted, but strangely, work out better. And sometimes the thing prayed for would not have been good. It's only in hindsight that we realise it. But, agonisingly, some things do not work out at all and we may question whether God is really there.

The answers may not be understood until eternity. This life on earth is only temporary because we are being prepared for eternity in which there is reward and judgement. The last book in the Bible has an incredible description of the future when there will be no more crying or pain. Perhaps then we will understand how close God has been throughout our life.

'He will wipe away every tear from their eyes. There will be no more death or mourning or crying or pain, for the old order of things has passed away.'[20]

Try telling God that you are willing to trust him – even with things that are confusing.

Evidence

Is it possible to have an evidence-based faith? The answer is yes. There is a lot of evidence.

One thing particularly stands out and is worth considering: the resurrection of Jesus. The historical documentary evidence surrounding this is convincing and open to examination. And the implications of the resurrection are significant: if it happened then all the rest is possible. If it didn't then, to put it bluntly, every Christian is deluded.

So what is the evidence?

The eyewitness accounts from the first century show that Jesus died as a result of crucifixion just outside Jerusalem. On several occasions he had said he would rise again so, to stop anyone stealing the body and starting a rumour, guards were put on the tomb.

But people started seeing him; many people and in different situations. Friends, sceptics and even opponents saw him alive. It is documented that as many as 500 saw him at one time. If this was all a rumour then the simplest way to put an end to it would have been to go to the tomb and produce his decomposing body.

But that was not possible. The tomb which had been protected by guards with a large stone in front of it was empty. Jesus was not there.

The historical evidence around this has been sifted and analysed over many years especially by those who wish to debunk it as a myth. But it still defies any reasonable explanation other than this: Jesus said he would rise again, and he did.